BIG BOOK OF
HORSES
TO COLOR

John Green

DOVER PUBLICATIONS, INC.
Mineola, New York

Bibliographical Note

This Dover edition, first published in 2006, contains all the plates shown in the following previously published Dover books by John Green: *Horses of the World Coloring Book* (1985); *Ponies of the World Coloring Book* (1999); *Favorite Horses Coloring Book* (2005); *Wonderful World of Horses Coloring Book* (2005).

International Standard Book Number

ISBN-13: 978-0-486-45178-7
ISBN-10: 0-486-45178-X

Manufactured in the United States by RR Donnelley
45178X08   2015
www.doverpublications.com

Favorite
HORSES

NOTE

For thousands of years horses have played an important part in human history. Strong and swift, they have pulled plows, hauled heavy loads, and carried soldiers into battle. Hitched to carts and carriages, they have provided transportation for people over the centuries. As racing horses and rodeo performers, these appealing animals have entertained countless thousands. Here are thirty different kinds of horses for you to color—from the beloved Shetland Pony to the swift and graceful Thoroughbred. Identifying captions give brief descriptions of each breed and its characteristics.

LIST OF HORSES

The **Andalusian** horse comes from the province of Andalusia in southern Spain. It has been known since ancient times as one of the best horses for use in battle.

Recognized by their spotted coats, **Appaloosas** were highly prized
by the Nez Perce Indians of the American Northwest.

The beautiful **Arabian** horse originated long ago in the deserts of the
Middle East, bred by tribes of wandering peoples called Bedouins.

The **Canadian** horse was first brought to Canada from France in the seventeenth century. Today, its strength and endurance make it a favorite with the Royal Canadian Mounted Police.

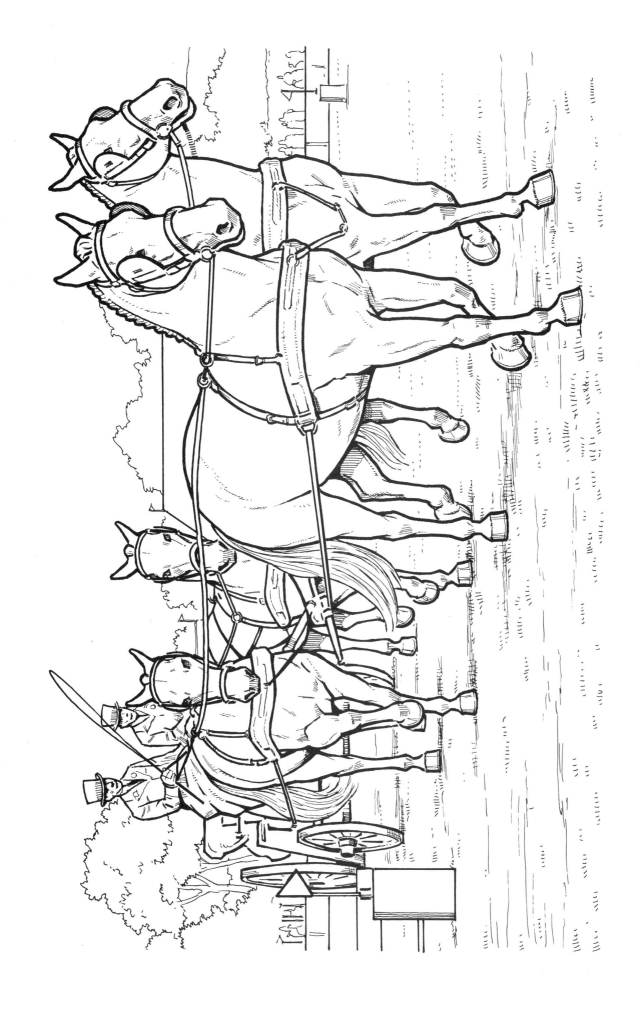

One of the oldest breeds of English horses, the **Cleveland Bay** is distinguished by its reddish-brown color, as well as its black mane, tail, and legs.

The **Clydesdale** is a large Scottish horse developed for hauling heavy loads.
A full-grown stallion can weigh up to 2,200 pounds.

The typical horse used by the New York City Mounted Police is a **Crossbreed**—a chestnut or bay gelding that can tolerate the noise and crowding of the city.

Crossbreed working horses play an important role in British royal ceremonies. They are mainly Cleveland Bays or **Windsor Greys.** The Greys are not a specific breed, but horses selected for appearance and temperament.

Known for its strength and spirit, the **Danish Warmblood** excels in such competitions as dressage (a series of carefully performed movements testing the horse's training and the rider's control) and cross-country events.

One of the oldest Russian riding horses, the **Don** breed was developed by the Cossack peoples of southern Russia.

A large, even-tempered animal, the British **Drum Horse** carries a rider
and two solid silver kettle drums during parades and events.

The **Friesian** horse originated centuries ago in the Netherlands when medieval knights used to ride them into battle. Today, these beautiful black horses are used to pull coaches and carriages on special occasions.

One of the best-known riding breeds in the world, the German **Hanoverian** is noble and well-proportioned, with natural balance and a calm disposition.

Known as far back as Viking times, the Danish **Knabstrup** (above) sports a beautiful, spotted coat. It is a calm and friendly horse, often found in circuses. One of the oldest horse breeds in Britain, the **Shetland Pony** (below) originated in the Shetland Islands off the coast of Scotland. Strong and gentle, it is among the most popular ponies in the world.

Exceptionally kind, intelligent, and willing to learn, Austrian **Lipizzaners** are famous
for their dressage routines (precise, dancelike movements guided by slight signals
from the rider) performed at the Spanish Riding School in Vienna.

Related to the Andalusian horse of Spain, the Portuguese **Lusitano**
is used in bullfighting and as a general riding horse.

The **Missouri Fox Trotter** was developed in the rugged Ozark Mountains during the nineteenth century by settlers who needed sure-footed, easy-riding horses that could travel long distances.

The **Morgan** horse began in eighteenth-century Massachusetts with a horse given to Justin Morgan, a Vermont schoolteacher. This American breed became widely known and admired for its strength, versatility, and all-around usefulness.

Still roaming the American West today, **Mustangs** are wild horses descended from horses brought by Spanish explorers in the 1500s.

Russia's most famous breed of horse, the **Orlov Trotter** began in the eighteenth century as a harness-racing horse known for speed and endurance.

Palomino horses boast a golden coat with white mane and tail and are popular in parades, rodeos, movies, and on television. "Palomino" is not actually a breed, but a color, and such horses as Morgans, American Saddlebreds, and Arabians can all be "palominos."

Bred for size, weight, and strength, the **Percheron** of France was a
favorite for hauling heavy loads around the farm.

Introduced to North America by European explorers, the swift and lively
Pinto was a popular mount with Native Americans.

The first breed native to the United States, the **Quarter Horse** was named for its ability to run very fast in a quarter-mile race. Its calm disposition and "cow sense" helped make it an excellent ranch horse as well.

American Saddlebreds are descended from British horses shipped to North America in the 1600s. Used for riding, plowing, pulling carriages, and other work, they combine an easy riding gait, strength, and stamina.

The **Selle Français,** or French Saddle Horse, is one of the finest sport horses in the world. This breed does very well in international show jumping.

Descended from the medieval "Great Horse," the large and powerful English **Shire** horse is ideal for hauling heavy loads or pulling a plow.

Dating back just over 200 years, **Standardbreds** were so named because early trotters were required to reach a certain "standard" for the mile distance. Today, the Standardbred is the fastest harness-racing horse in the world.

Developed in eastern England to handle heavy farmwork, the **Suffolk Punch** breed of draft horse boasts great strength, endurance, and an easygoing temperament.

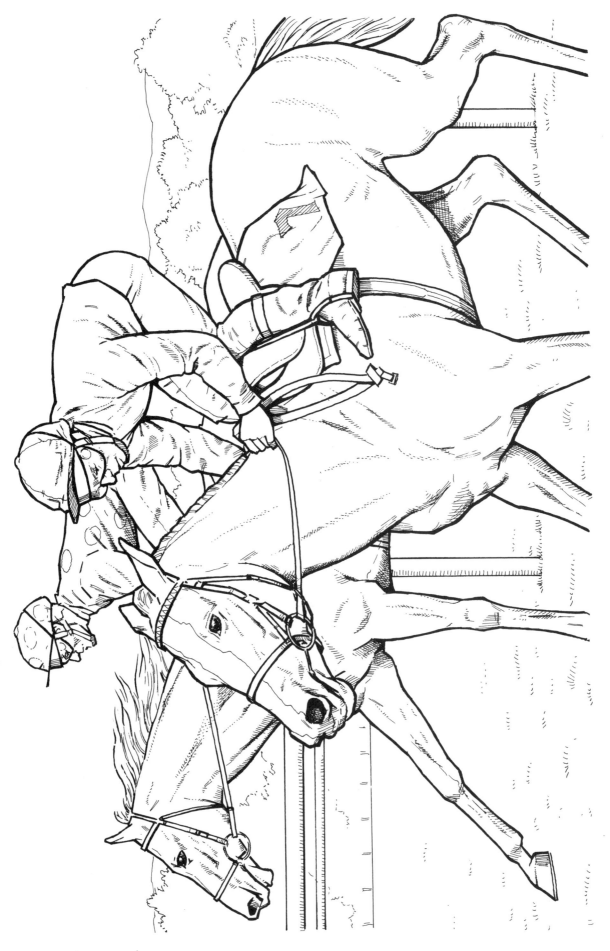

Properly known as the English Running Horse, the **Thoroughbred** is the fastest of all horses, capable of running for a mile at almost 40 miles per hour.

HORSES
OF THE WORLD

Note and Captions by
Robert Stephen Kendal

Note

The horse is an integral part of our lives, honored everywhere in the familiar images of the patient, hard-working farm horse, the swift racehorse, the nimble circus horse, and the valiant steed of the knight in armor. Despite their diversity, all horses belong to the single species *Equus caballus*. There are, however, three basic types. The *light breeds* are physically streamlined and possess speed, stamina, and spirit. Sometimes called *warmbloods*, the light breeds are used for riding, driving, racing, and various other sports, competitions, and recreations. Certain types of light breeds are sometimes separated into a category of their own, the coach horses. The *heavy breeds* (sometimes called *coldbloods*) are massive and bulky and are used for draft, farm work, and other heavy labor. They generally are of a more placid disposition than the light horses and are bred for strength rather than speed or agility. *Ponies* form the third general type. Although ponies are often ridden by children, that is no indication of the age of the horses themselves. Ponies sometimes stand as little as 5 hands high (a *hand* equals 4 inches) when fully grown. By convention, a pony is any breed of which the fully grown horses measure less than 14.2 hands high. (Measurement, again by widely accepted convention, is from the withers, that is, the top of the shoulders; by another convention, the "decimal" point is not a decimal point at all, the number following this point being read as inches. Therefore, 14.2 hands should be interpreted as 56 inches plus 2 inches, that is, 58 inches high at the withers.) Used for many purposes, ponies are as a rule sturdy, sure-footed, and lively.

Colors of horses range from pure white to gray, yellow, brown, reddish brown, and black. Describing a horse's coloration, however, is not a simple matter, since these colors are found in an enormous number of shades, combinations, and patterns, many of which have their own special names. A number of these names have been defined in a special glossary, below. When referring to a horse's color, the *points* indicate the mane, the muzzle, the tail, the lower legs, and the tips of the ears. To further complicate the matter of identifying a horse's coloring, the legs are sometimes identified separately from the other points, for they are frequently white, at least up to the knees, in cases where no other white is permitted in a specific breed. The face sometimes also has a patch of white that is considered separately.

The following 42 drawings present a broad spectrum of the fascinating, variegated world of horses, including breeds and types from Europe, Asia, and both North and South America.

Glossary of Color Terms

Bay: Brown or reddish shades with black points.
Chestnut: Shades ranging from reddish brown to golden yellow, without black points.
Dun: Grayish yellow with black points.
Odd-colored: Patches of white, black, and another color.
Piebald: Patches of black and white.
Roan: Any solid color intermixed with white hairs throughout. Blue roan denotes a black coat with white hairs, plus some red hairs. Strawberry roan is chestnut with white hairs.
Skewbald: Patches of white and any brownish color.
Sorrel: Bright chestnut, often with white mane and tail.

1. Until quite recently, **Przewalski's Horse** (or the **Mongolian** or **Asiatic Wild Horse**) roamed wild in western Mongolia, the last true wild horse. An extremely tough, hardy animal, Przewalski's Horse stands about 13.1 hands high and is usually dun (sometimes bay, brown, or black).

2. Riding this **Arab** horse is one of Napoleon's cuirassiers (1812). Often used to improve other breeds, Arab horses are renowned for their speed, spirit, and endurance. The Arab is bay or chestnut, or occasionally gray or brown, and stands about 14.3 or 15 hands high.

3. The **Shire** is the great heavy breed of England, a descendant in part from the medieval Great Horse. The Shire is the tallest horse in the world (17 hands or more) and one of the strongest. Any solid color is acceptable, offset by white markings, and with an abundance of fine feather (hairs over the hoofs).

4. The **Quarter-Horse** is the oldest breed in the United States, so named because it was originally tested by racing it over a quarter of a mile. Standing at 15.3 hands and found in solid colors, particularly chestnut, the adaptable Quarter-Horse is a favorite for ranch work and is altogether the most popular native breed.

5. The **Camarguais** is a hardy gray pony of the salt-marsh plain of the Rhône delta, in southern France. It is often ridden by *gardians* (the French version of the American cowboy) to capture wild bulls for the bullring. The Camarguais ponies also roam wild in the region, as they have done for centuries.

6. The **Friesian** horse, of Dutch origin, is one of Europe's oldest breeds. Standing 15 hands high and always black, the Friesian is a reliable, good-tempered horse for riding, driving, and performing. A fourteenth-century knight in full armor is shown riding the Friesian in this drawing.

7. The **Morgan** is the oldest American breed that can be traced to an individual horse: Justin Morgan, the namesake of its owner, a Massachusetts schoolteacher. The horse Justin Morgan was foaled in 1793, and since then its descendants have become one of America's most popular breeds. The Morgan, standing at about 15 hands, is strong, fast, graceful, and good-tempered. Colors are black, brown, chestnut, or bay.

8. Another old and distinguished breed is the **Holstein**. Like other fine German breeds, it is named for its region of origin. Outbreeding the native Marsh Horse of the Schleswig-Holstein region with foreign stock gradually produced a tall (16.1 hands), sturdy animal with a high-stepping action, internationally prized for riding and competitions. Holsteins are colored black, brown, or bay.

9. The **Albino** is not a true albino, a genetic type of animal that has pink eyes and is a frail creature. The Albino horse has blue, brown, or "glass" eyes and is a perfectly normal horse in every respect. An American light breed registered for its all-white coat, the Albino may be of any height or physique; it is used for riding.

10. A horse ridden to the hunt must possess agility and stamina, must respond quickly to its rider's commands, and must be able to jump fences and other obstacles without hesitation. The **Hunter** is not actually a distinct breed but may be any horse with these qualities useful in hunting.

11. The **Pinto**, a favorite of American Indians, is one of several types in America classified primarily by color. Pintos are usually piebald, sometimes skewbald. They are versatile horses popular for riding and ranchwork.

12. The **Andalusian** is a large, graceful Spanish horse of the type brought to the New World. An athletic, intelligent, and obedient animal, the Andalusian is often used in *dressage*, the performance of complicated precision movements in response to subtle commands of the rider. The Andalusian comes in a variety of colors and stands about 16 hands high.

13. The Spanish brought horses to the New World in 1519. There the domesticated animal often escaped to run wild. After centuries, many of the wild horses were redomesticated and bred. One result of this sequence of events was the creation of the Argentinian **Criollo**, the horse of the *gaucho* (South American cowboy). The Criollo is a smallish breed, almost of pony size, and is found in most colors.

49

14. The cob is another horse that is not a breed but a type. Cobs are stocky, short-legged horses that possess great stamina and strength for their size, and are well suited to riding, driving, and general work. The Irish are great lovers of horses and have cultivated many fine breeds and types, of which the **Irish Cob** shown here is one.

15. Originating in the Shetland and Orkney Islands of Scotland, the **Shetland Pony** has become the most familiar pony in the world. The strong, hardy, sure-footed, and friendly Shetland is popular as a children's riding horse. It may be anywhere from 6.2 to 14 hands in height, and its colors may be black, brown, piebald, skewbald, or odd-colored.

16. The **Mustang** is one of the descendants of the horses introduced to the New World by the Spanish. Still often roaming wild in the Western United States, the Mustang was often used by American Indians and is still a favorite wherever beauty, speed, and endurance are valued.

17. The English **Suffolk Punch** is among the smallest of the heavy breeds (15.2 to 16.2 hands high) but is muscular and powerful, gentle and long-lived. Its color is always chestnut.

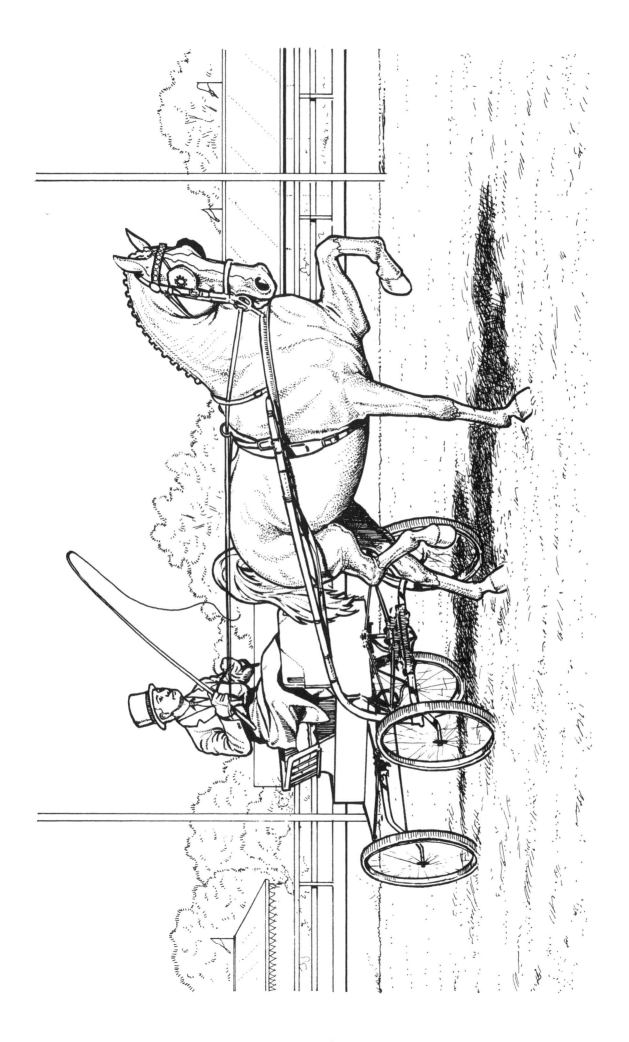

18. The **Hackney** is an elegant, high-stepping, but nervous driving horse of eighteenth-century British origin. Now used mostly in shows and competitions, the Hackney is about 15 hands high and may be of any dark color, occasionally roan.

19. The **Thoroughbred**, the most famous, the most honored, and the most influential of all breeds of horse, originated in England in the eighteenth century. Standing at about 16 hands and always in solid colors, the Thoroughbred is a sleek, sinewy animal familiar on race tracks around the world. Most horses bred for speed will possess at least some Thoroughbred blood.

20. One of a number of horses widely associated with the American West, the **Palomino** is bred primarily for color, which must be golden, with a white or "flax" (an off-white) mane and tail. This versatile horse stands from 14 to 16 hands high.

21. The **Lusitano** is one of a number of distinguished Portuguese breeds. This tough, hardy, lightweight gray horse stands 15.1 hands high and is favored for the bullring.

22. A cutting horse must be capable of separating an animal from a herd, which the **Canadian Cutting Horse** does supremely well. A type rather than a breed, this fast, intelligent horse stands at 15.2 to 16 hands and may be almost any color.

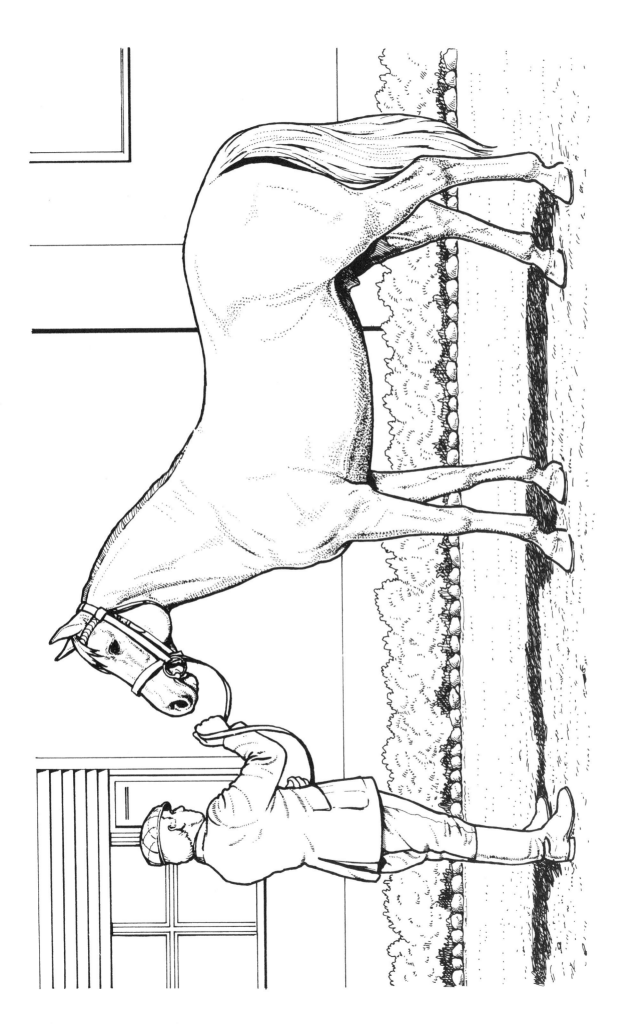

23. Many of the finest horses come from Eastern Europe. The major influence on Hungary's excellent breeds has been Arabian. The gray **Shagya Arab**, standing about 15 hands high, is a splendid animal, used in military service and for general riding and driving.

61

24. The **Lipizzaner** is the horse specially bred for use in the Spanish Riding School in Vienna, renowned for the excellence of its *Haute École* equitation, the most elaborate form of dressage. This extremely athletic gray or white horse (15.1 hands high) can be trained to perform the most complicated and specialized movements.

25. The **Falabella** is one of the smallest ponies in the world. Named after its breeder, Julio Falabella of Argentina, this exceedingly diminutive horse can stand as little as 5 hands high when fully grown. Naturally, these tiny Falabellas are not intended for riding but they make charming pets. Any color is acceptable.

26. The American **Standardbred**, so called because it was bred to certain standards, is the horse used in harness racing. Shown here is a pacer, a horse trained to move forward both legs on one side at the same time (an ordinary trot involves moving forward the front leg on one side and the rear leg on the other side at the same time). Standardbreds come in solid colors and stand about 15.2 hands high. They make fine riding as well as racing horses, being of less nervous temperament than their cousins the Thoroughbreds.

27. The **Hanoverian,** one of Germany's most distinguished breeds, was developed gradually over centuries. The addition of Arab and other blood to that of the medieval Great War Horse produced a strong, tall (16 hands), splendid animal suitable for both general riding and formal competitions.

28. The **Saddlebred** is America's finest show horse. The five-gaited type of Saddlebred is able to perform excellent versions of the usual walk, trot, and canter, as well as two other less-common gaits in which each foot touches the ground separately. This intelligent, handsome, and exceedingly graceful animal stands about 15.2 hands high and is found in black, brown, gray, or chestnut.

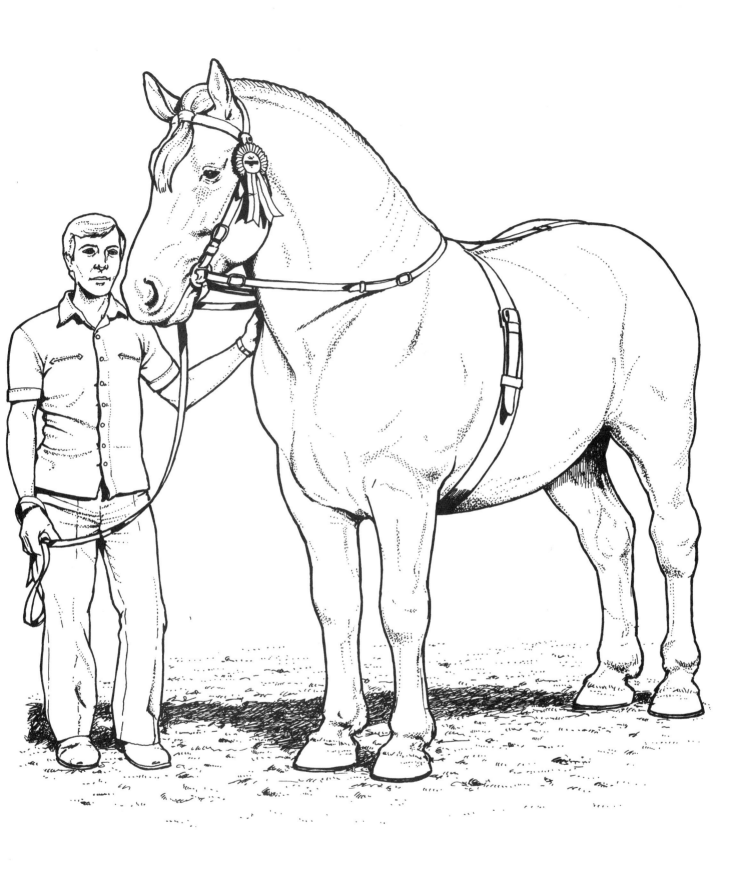

29. The **Percheron** is easily the most famous French draft horse. Beautiful specimens of this noble, powerful, docile animal are now prized the world over. Percherons are gray or black and stand some 16.1 hands high.

30. The **Galiceno** is a versatile North American pony standing at about 12.2 hands and usually found in bay, black, or dun. It possesses a natural running walk.

31. The massive **Italian Heavy Draft Horse** is Italy's great contribution to the heavy breeds. A fast, strong horse used widely in agricultural work, it stands 15.2 hands high and is found in roan or sorrel.

32. The **Appaloosa** was developed by the Nez Percé Indians in the American West. Its color pattern—white with black spots—is familiar the world over. These sturdy, beautiful animals make excellent general-purpose horses. There is also a mottled blue roan and gray color type.

33. The **American Shetland Pony** was developed from the Scottish Shetland. The second most popular horse in the United States, the American Shetland is an excellent jumper and a favorite riding horse for children. It is a more slender animal than its European counterpart.

34. Sweden's great contribution to the dressage arena is the **Swedish Halfbred**, noted for its straight action (as seen here). Of highly mixed Oriental and European pedigree blood, the Swedish Halfbred stands 16.1 hands high and is found in solid colors.

35. The **French Saddle Horse,** or [Cheval de] **Selle Français,** is one of the finest examples of France's many conscientious breeding programs. This first-rate competition horse stands 16.1 hands high and may be of any solid color.

36. An American breed of recent origin, the **Tennessee Walking Horse** is a gentle and extremely smooth-riding horse with a special running walk for which it is famous. A popular show horse, it is bred in solid colors and stands at 15.2 hands.

37. The **Knabstrup**, one of a number of fine Danish breeds, is widely favored as a circus horse. Its coloration is distinctive—Appaloosa-like black spots on a roan base. It stands some 15.3 hands high.

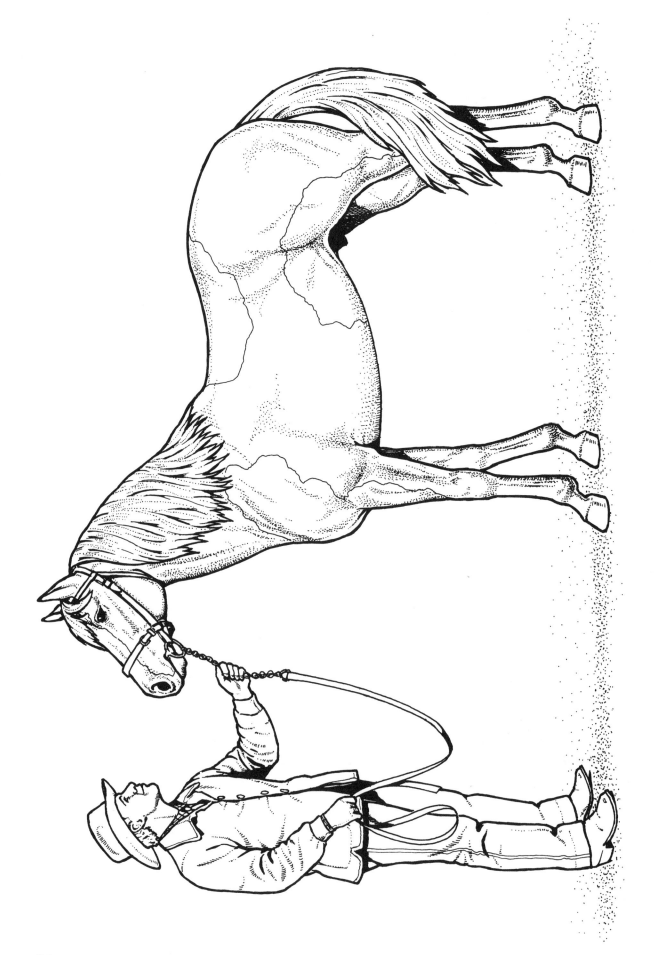

38. The **Paso Fino** of Puerto Rico is an unusual horse that is capable of special gaits. Little larger than a pony (14.3 hands), this spirited performer is found in most colors It has become very popular in the United States.

39. The **Anglo-Arab** (the drawing shows a mare with foal) is neither English nor Arab, but French, although it does possess both Arab and English Thoroughbred blood. Found in solid colors and standing at about 16 hands, this speedy animal makes an exceptional racehorse.

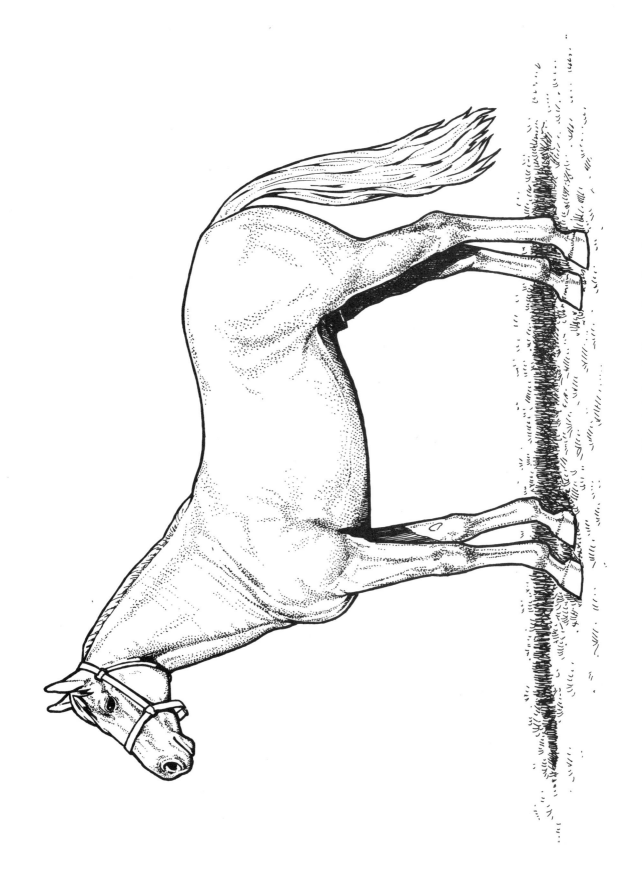

40. The **Oldenburg** is exceptionally tall for a light breed of horse, the tallest of many such breeds to come out of Germany. Used for both riding and driving, it is 16.3 hands high.

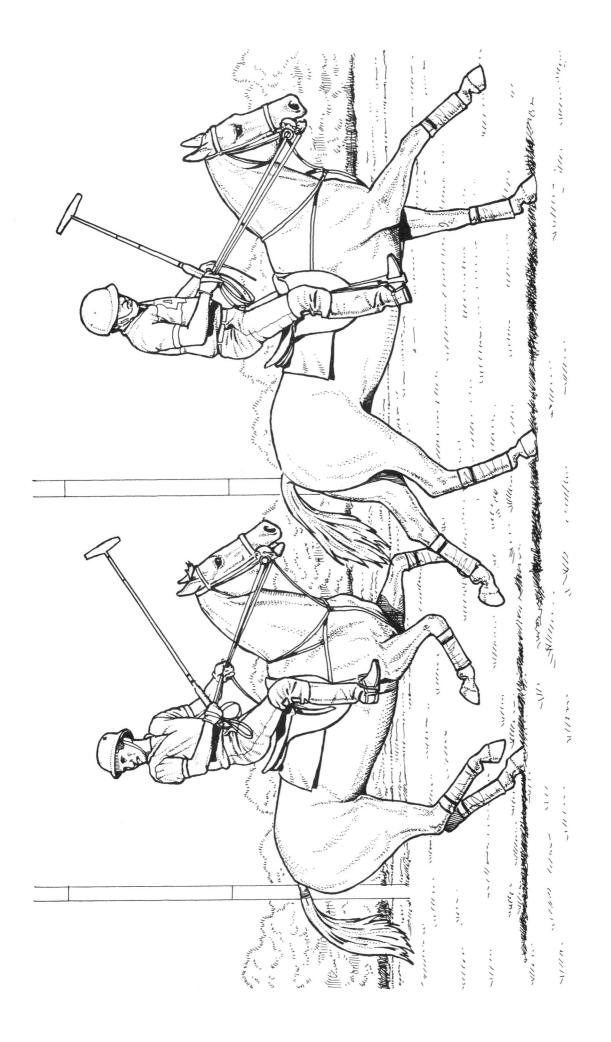

41. Polo places heavy demands on the horses used to play it. The **Polo Pony**, standing from 13 to 14 hands high, must be fast and agile and possess stamina; it must respond instantly to the commands of its rider. In recent years, Argentina has produced the world's finest polo players, as well as some of the best Polo Ponies.

42. The **Pony of the Americas** is a cross between the Appaloosa horse and the Shetland Pony, with the distinctive qualities of both. It is a popular children's riding pony.

Wonderful World of
HORSES

NOTE

Horses take hold of our imagination when they gallop across the plains, whinnying into the wind. They evoke a timeless romance with their mere presence and have done more to change human history than any other domestic animal. Perhaps these are some of the reasons why so many people have had their hearts captured by these magnificent creatures. Now John Green skillfully portrays the legendary grace and beauty of these animals in this collection of thirty illustrations. Handsome equinnes—from Clydesdales to show horses—are depicted in the wild and at work and brief captions supplement an impressive panorama of one of the world's best-loved and most highly prized animals.

Running free

A real winner

Gallop free

Freckles

Standing tall

A wild ride

A good trotter

Rugged rider

A Clydesdale

91

Home sweet home

Majestic stallion

Horsing around

Desert paradise

Best friends

In the Canadian Rockies

Three of a kind

Show jumping

Faithful friend

River dance

Time for a drink

Fox hunting

A noble steed

Working the land

Spirited siblings

Swift and sure-footed

Way out west

A shady resting-place

Dressage

Free as the wind

The world at a gallop

PONIES

OF THE WORLD

NOTE

A pony is a small horse, less than 14 hands high. A "hand" is 4 inches, or about 10 centimeters, long. The height is determined by measuring the distance from the highest point of a horse's withers (the ridge between the shoulder bones) in a perpendicular line to the ground. Polo ponies and cow ponies are often several inches taller than the official height limit, yet they are still called ponies.

Ponies, which tend to be sturdier and hardier than horses, often live in the wild where they endure harsh weather and survive on meager diets. Because ponies are usually gentle and intelligent, for centuries people have used them for work and pleasure. The pony's small size and generally docile disposition has made it an ideal mount for children. In some parts of the world, however, adults ride ponies and use them to carry or pull heavy loads.

Color glossary

bay: reddish shades on the body; black mane, tail, and lower legs (known as points).

black: true black with no light areas.

brown: black with light areas at the muzzle, eyes, and inside of the legs.

chestnut: pure or reddish brown with points the same or lighter color.

dorsal, or eel stripe: a stripe running down a horse's neck, and along its back, sometimes to the tip of its tail; usually black, brown, or chestnut color; found mostly on dun-colored animals.

dun: gray-yellow with a black dorsal stripe, black mane and tail; sometimes there are zebra stripes on the legs and a crosswise stripe on the withers.

piebald: a horse with black and white patches over its body, sometimes including its tail.

roan: any color with white hairs mixed throughout, lightening the effect.

skewbald: a horse covered with patches of white and any color, except black.

sorrel: light chestnut, often with white mane and tail.

Sable Island Pony. Descended from horses that were brought to Nova Scotia from France, the Sable Island pony has roamed semi-wild since the 18th century. The harsh climate of the island has forced this pony to become incredibly hardy. Its coat may be gray, brown, black, or chestnut. If domesticated young, it is docile. It is used for riding and pulling light loads.

Assateague and Chincoteague Ponies. These ponies are believed to be descended from horses that survived a shipwreck in the early days of the American colonies. The island of Assateague, off the coasts of Virginia and Maryland, is uninhabited by humans. Here the ponies live in the wild. Each year, at the end of July, ponies are herded across the channel to the island of Chincoteague, where they are auctioned. Although they are known to be rebellious and stubborn, these ponies are used for riding and pulling light loads. Their coats can be almost any color, although piebald and skewbald are most common.

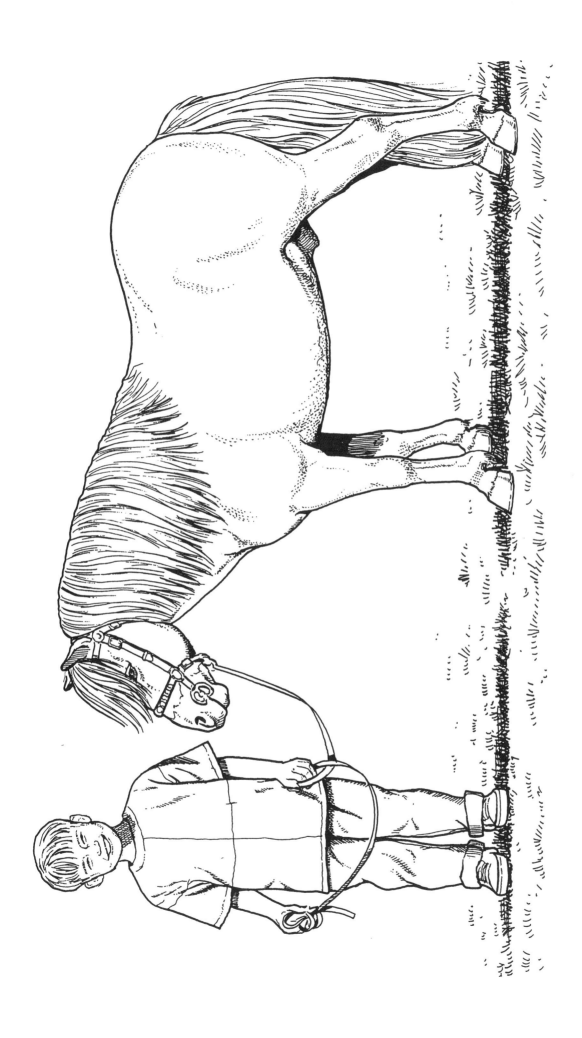

Shetland Pony. The Shetland pony is from the Shetland and Orkney islands, north of Scotland. While fossils suggest that this pony dates back to the Bronze Age, some experts believe that it was brought by a ship in the Spanish Armada during the 16th century. Standing 9 to 10 hands, it is one of the smallest of all ponies, and may be the strongest of all horses in relation to its size. Hearty and long lived, it is also the most popular breed. Because it can be stubborn, this pony needs firm training. Shetlands with coats that are chestnut, bay, and black are popular for show, Shetlands with piebald and skewbald coats tend to be chosen for children.

American Shetland Pony. As a result of different breeding conditions in the United States, the American Shetland is a lighter, more refined version of the Shetland pony from the United Kingdom.

Pony of the Americas. The result of breeding a Shetland pony with an Appaloosa in the 1960s, the Pony of the Americas grows to 12.1 hands. Its coat is usually a dark spotted pattern on roan or white. Versatile, swift, and an excellent jumper, this pony is popular for competition, racing, and long distance riding. It's a docile pony, ideal for children.

Galiçeno Pony. Descended from the Garrano, this pony was brought to Mexico by Spanish *conquistadors* in the 16th century. Today it is used in Mexico for carrying packs, draft, and farm work. Its coat may be bay, black, or chestnut, with piebald, skewbald, and albino not permitted. Known to be gentle, intelligent, and courageous, the Galiçeno has been imported to the United States since 1950 where it has proved to be a fine jumper in events for children.

Falabella Pony. At 34 inches high, or 86 centimeters, the Falabella pony is the smallest breed in the world. Bred by the Falabella family at their ranch near Argentina, it is docile and intelligent. It's a popular riding and harness pony for children because it is so strong for its size. Graceful and attractive, it comes in all colors.

Connemara Pony. The Connemara pony is an ancient Celtic breed, one of the earliest inhabitants of the British Isles. For centuries, the tough, handsome Connemara has run wild on the west coast of Ireland. With its compact body and short legs, it is known for its stamina and staying power. Docile and intelligent, it is used for riding and driving. The Connemara pony is usually gray, but may also be black, bay, brown, dun, roan, or chestnut.

Dales Pony. The Dales pony, a native of northern England, has a strong frame that enables it to pull heavy loads. In the 19th century, it was used to carry lead from the mines to the docks. A harness pony today, it is popular for work on small farms, especially in Scotland. Many Dales ponies are jet black, followed by bay, brown, and gray. They all have thick manes and tails.

Dartmoor Pony. An indigenous, mountain breed, the Dartmoor pony roams wild over the high, craggy hills of Dartmoor, in the extreme southwest of England. If handled when young, it will become an excellent riding pony, especially for a child. Small and compact, it is remarkably long lived. With its tail set high and full, the Dartmoor pony is usually black, bay, or brown.

Fell Pony. At the end of the 19th century, the Fell pony roamed wild over the barren moors of northern England. Like the Dales pony, the Fell pony was once used to carry lead from the mines to the docks. But while the Dales pony is now favored for carrying packs, the Fell pony is preferred for riding. Its coat is usually black, with no white markings, but it may also be dark brown, dark bay, gray, or dun.

Exmoor Pony. The Exmoor pony, descended from the native British wild horse, continues to roam the English moors of Cornwall, Devon, and Somerset. This pony remains small and hearty, which is thought to be its ancient, aboriginal state. If taken into captivity at a young age, and gently treated, it becomes a lovable, good mount. Its coloring, which may be brown, bay, or dun, is without white. When full grown, this pony may reach up to 12.2 hands.

Avelignese Pony. Although there is little known about the earliest origins of the Avelignese pony, its history can be traced back to the Middle Ages. Originating in Italy, it is considered a breed of inter- national importance. Its coat is usually chestnut or golden, with forelock, mane, and tail a lighter shade. There is often a white blaze or understated white marking on its head.

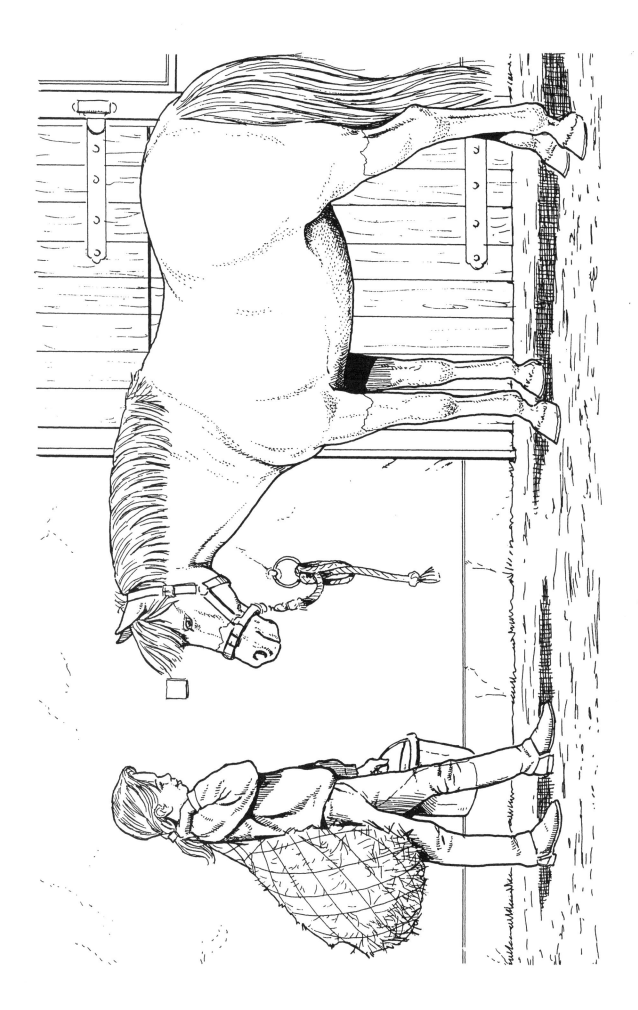

Welsh Pony. The Welsh pony is a strong harness and riding pony with considerable spirit, ability, and a kind temperament. It is known for its beautiful stride, at both a trot and a gallop. In Wales it is predominantly gray, and dark, solid colors; cream and buckskin are popular in the United States. Its height may be from 12 to 13.2 hands.

Welsh Cob. Descended from the Welsh Mountain pony, the Welsh Cob has inherited its hardy constitution. At 14 to 15.1 hands, the Welsh Cob is ideal for carrying heavier riders, even over rough and difficult terrain. Huskier cobs are impressively strong, noted for pulling substantial loads. As with the Welsh Mountain pony, the coat of the Welsh Cob may be bay, brown, black, roan, or chestnut. It is occasionally dun or cream, but never piebald or skewbald.

Welsh Mountain Pony. This little pony, its height under 12 hands, still roams wild, or semi-wild, over the mountains and moors of Wales. Its intelligence, courage, endurance, and beauty make it a favorite of adults and children alike. Because of its small size, the Welsh Mountain Pony was once in great demand in coal mines. Today it is prized for riding and as foundation stock for breeding children's ponies. The dominant coat color is gray, followed by brown, chestnut, and many other colors. Only piebald and skewbald are not allowed.

Camargue Pony. This pony, which lives in the wilds of the Camargue, the salt marsh delta of the Rhône in France, remains unchanged since Roman times. *Guardiens,* or cowboys, ride them in pursuit of the wild black bulls that are exported to the bullrings of Spain.

The coat of the Camargue is usually gray, with bay or brown occurring rarely. Facing extinction towards the middle of the 20th century, this breed has had its own register since 1967.

Palomino Pony. The Palomino is registered by color because it does not yet breed true to type. Cortez, in Mexico in 1519, presented a horse of this color to Juan de Palomino. Known today as "the golden horse of the West," Palominos were rediscovered in 1848, after the Mexican War, when the United States took possession of California. Standing 14 to 16 hands, the Palomino is used for riding, driving, and stock work. The pony version is found only in Britain.

Haflinger Pony. Originally from the Tyrol, the Haflinger pony is a mountain horse who carries its head close to the ground as it climbs. Strong and sure-footed, it excels at carrying and pulling heavy loads, and has been employed in the mountains to work in forestry and agriculture. Its average height is under 14 hands; its color is usually dark bay or black.

Dolmen Pony. The Dolmen pony, from Westphalia, is bred on the estate of the Duke of Croy. The only native German pony, it is excellent for riding. The Dolmen pony stands at 12.3 hands with coat colors that are black, brown, or dun.

Konik Pony. Konik, which means "small horse" in Polish, refers to several native breeds in Poland. With Arabic and Celtic ancestors, this pony is valued for its stamina, hardiness, and speed. A very popular type of Konik pony comes from the Baltic region where it does agricultural work. The Konik is a mid-sized, good-natured pony whose coat color may be palomino, gray, or blue dun, usually with a dorsal stripe.

Hucul Pony. The Hucul has roamed the wilds of Poland's Carpathians for centuries, retaining its primitive features. Descended from the Tarpan, the Hucul was first bred formally in the 19th century. It is solidly built, standing 12 to 13 hands. Hardy and undemanding, it is used for pulling and carrying light loads, as well as for farm work. The most common colors are bay, palomino, dun, mouse dun, and gray.

Sorraia Pony. One of the first ponies to be domesticated, the Sorraia is strong and tractable enough to carry packs, to herd, and to work in agriculture. Standing about 13 hands, the Sorraia pony comes from Portugal, where it lives in the wild. Changes in its natural habitat now threaten its existence. Its coat colors may be dun, gray, or palomino, with a dorsal stripe down its back, and zebra markings on its legs.

Tarpan Pony. With origins dating back to the Ice Age, the Tarpan is the ancestor of all the lightly-built breeds now in existence. Today, herds of Tarpan ponies roam wild in the forests of Poland. They are not thought to be purebred, however, because the last true Tarpan died in captivity in 1887. Standing at about 13 hands, they are brave, independent, and difficult to train. The Tarpan's coat may be mouse dun, yellow dun, or palomino. It has a black dorsal stripe down the center of its back, a black mane and tail, and black or zebra-marked legs.

Garrano Pony. Ponies of this very old breed resemble horses depicted in cave paintings from the Paleolithic era. Originating in Portugal, along the Spanish border, until recently the Garrano pony was used for traditional trotting races. Today it is utilized as a riding and pack pony, and for farm work. A small pony, it stands from 10 to 12 hands and has a quiet, docile temperament. Its coat is chestnut.

Fjord Pony. Retaining the characteristics of its Ice Age ancestors, the Norwegian Fjord pony was used by Vikings during times of war, as shown in rock and cave paintings. Present day heavy draft breeds in western Europe are thought to be descended from this strong, stocky pony. Standing about 13 to 14 hands, it is used today as a riding and pack pony, and for light draft and farm work. Usually dun-colored with a black dorsal stripe and a black and silver mane, the Fjord pony is gentle, but stubborn.

Iceland Pony. The Iceland pony is descended from two types of ponies that were brought to Iceland by settlers; the Norwegians arrived in 874, followed soon after by the Irish. For a thousand years, this pony provided the only means of transportation on Iceland. Short and stocky, it is extremely hardy, with exceptionally sharp eyesight. Because the Iceland pony is born with a unique homing ability, there is a custom of turning a pony loose after a long trip; it usually returns home within 24 hours. Although gentle and friendly, the Iceland pony is stubborn, independent, and difficult to train.

142

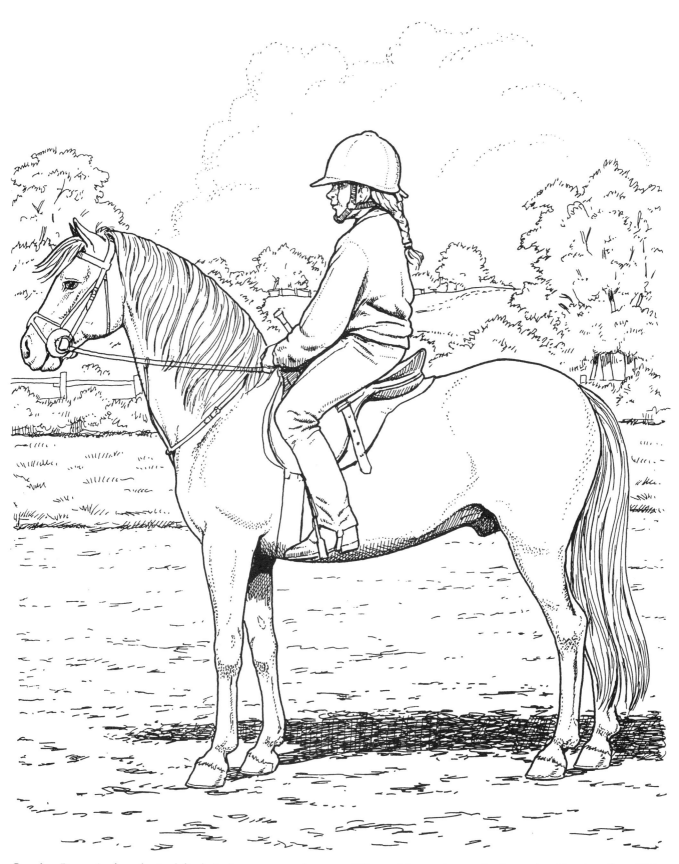

Caspian Pony. Archaeological finds in Iran suggest that ancestors of the Caspian pony may have been domesticated by the Mesopotamians around 3000 B.C. Thought to have become extinct by the 10th century, in 1965, a number of these ponies were discovered living in Iran's Elburz Mountains and along the Caspian Sea. This docile pony is a good riding horse and an excellent jumper. Its coat may be chestnut, bay, or gray; a few have white markings on their heads and legs.

Bosnian Pony. This durable pony is so important for farm work that its breeding is closely monitored by the state. It is also used for carrying packs, light draft, and riding. Standing at 12 to 14 hands, the Bosnian pony may be bay, dun, brown, black, or chestnut.

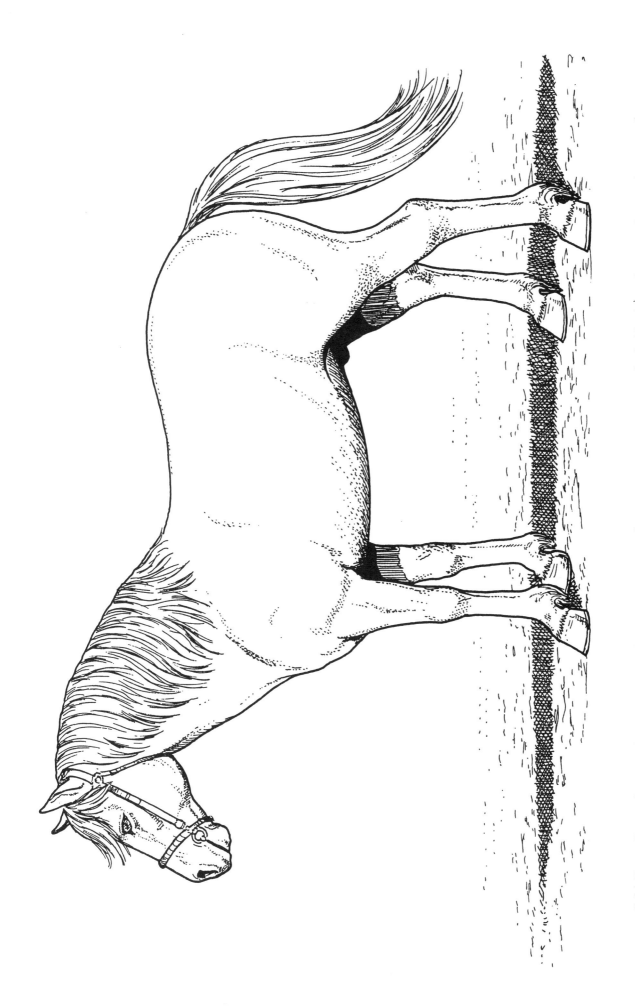

Spiti Pony. From the Himalayas in India, the Spiti is a rugged mountain pony that thrives only in the cold climate. The ponies carry huge loads up and down winding mountain paths. Usually tied together in a long line, the ponies walk with their heads down. Despite appearing to be half asleep, they are always alert enough to nip at whoever or whatever gets in their way. About 12 hands high, the Spiti often has a gray coat.

New Forest Pony. The New Forest pony roams the 60,000 acre New Forest in southern England which, in reality, is a sparse grazing land of scrub and heather. In order to survive under such desolate conditions, these ponies have become frugal eaters who can endure harsh weather. The present breed was developed in the mid-19th century when Queen Victoria sent an Arab stallion to live in the New Forest for 8 years. Intelligent, courageous, and willing, the New Forest pony is used for light draft work, polo, and other equestrian competitions. The most common coat color for this pony is gray or brown. All colors are permitted, except piebald and skewbald.

146

Skyros Pony. From the Greek island of Skyros, this pony is one of the few breeds that has not interbred. Quiet and trustworthy, it is used as a pack animal, for farm work, and as a riding pony for children. Considered unattractive in its wild state, its appearance improves greatly with proper food and care. Its height is approximately 10 hands. Its coat may be dun, brown, or gray.

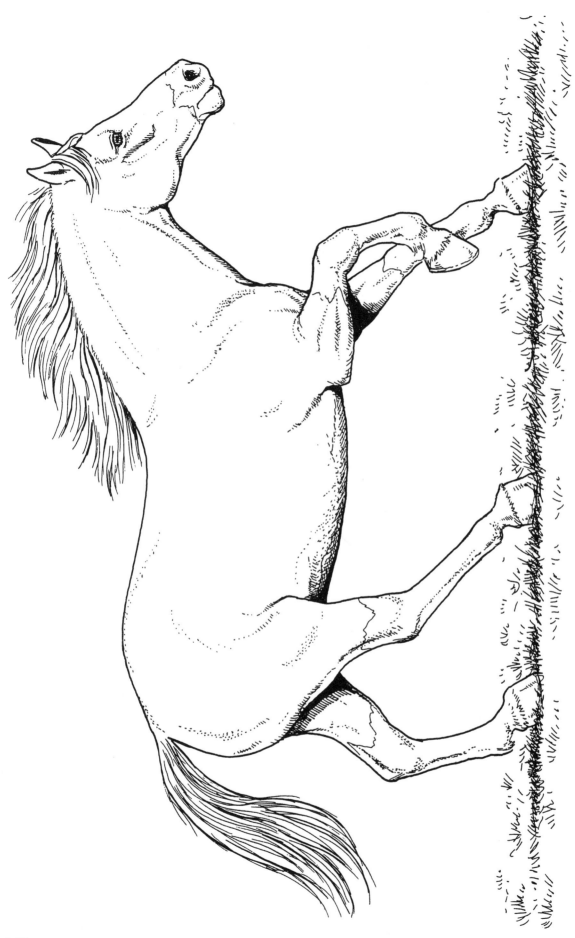

Zemaituka Pony. This pony, from western Lithuania, has ancient beginnings. Renowned for its staying power and ability to survive hardship, it has been mentioned as far back as the 13th century when it carried warriors on raids deep into Russia. Today it is used for farm work and light draft. From 13 to 15 hands high, it may be dun color with a light tail and mane, as well as mouse color or bay. A dorsal or eel stripe extends to its tail.

Bashkirsky Pony. A very old breed from the Baltic region, Bashkirsky mares have long been milked for koumiss, a medicinal and alcoholic drink. Standing 13 to 14 hands tall, this strong pony is used for riding and light draft. There are two types of Bashkirsky ponies; the smaller and lighter mountain type is better suited to riding, while the heavier, steppes type is used for pulling a troika (a Russian vehicle with 3 horses abreast). Its coat is usually bay, chestnut, dun, or palomino.

Mongolian Pony. Of ancient origin, this pony is kept and bred in huge numbers by nomad Mongolian tribes who do not provide them with any special care or food. The region where they live is extremely inhospitable, so the ponies that adapted over the centuries have become hardy. The most valued Mongolian pony is the Wuchumutsin who has the advantage of being reared in fertile pastures. The coat of the Mongolian pony may be brown, black, dun or palomino.

Viatka Pony. Originating in the Baltic states, this breed is descended from the Konik pony. Energetic and willing, it is used for light farm work. Because it has a short stride, the Viatka pony does especially well on snow covered ground. Its coat may be bay, gray, or roan. A coat that is dun, mouse dun, or palomino is usually accompanied by an eel stripe, zebra markings on the legs, a black mane and tail.

Batak Pony. Originating in Indonesia and Sumatra, the Batak pony averages about 11.3 hands, although some reach the height of 12.2 hands. Bred from a native pony and an Arabian, its physique is comparatively refined and well formed. Of gentle temperament and modest needs, it is an excellent pony for agricultural and transportation work. Most have brown coats, although many are skewbald.

Highland Pony. The Highland pony is the largest and the strongest of Great Britain's moor land and mountain breeds. Found in the highlands of Scotland and a few adjacent islands, its origins can be traced back to the Ice Age. With a strong and sturdy build, it has been used in the mountains to hunt deer. Its coat may be black, brown, dun, gray, and many other colors.

Manipur Pony. The Manipur pony is mentioned as far back as the 7th century when the king of Manipur, in India, introduced polo which was played on ponies bred in his state. Although polo had long been known in Asia, English colonials first saw polo being played in India during the mid-19th century and introduced it in Europe. The quick, maneuverable Manipur pony has a coat that is usually bay, brown, gray, or chestnut.

Hackney Pony. First bred in England in the 1860s, the Hackney pony is a smaller edition of the Hackney horse. A high stepper with a graceful stride, the Hackney pony was once used to pull farmers to market. Today this handsome pony is often seen jumping in the show ring, a sport at which it excels. The pony has a long neck, good shoulders, and a compact body. Its colors are usually bay, brown, or black.

Gotland Pony. Since the Stone Age, this Swedish pony has run wild on the island of Gotland in the Baltic Sea. It is sometimes called "Skogsruss," which means "little horse in the woods," or "little goat," because it is so sure-footed. Although this hardy pony tends to be obstinate, it is used for light farm work, in trotting races, and as a children's pony. Standing from 12 to 13 hands high, its coat may be bay, brown, black, chestnut, gray, dun, palomino, or mouse dun.

Rocky Mountain Pony. Bred by Sam Tuttle of Stout Springs, Kentucky, this new breed was first registered in 1986. Calm and kind, this pony is sure-footed over rough ground. Of Spanish origin, it can measure up to 14.3 hands high. It's an all around pony that is a good choice for work on the farm, in the harness, or with a saddle.

INDEX OF PONIES